ANIMAL ARCHITECTS
SPIDERS

by Karen

pogo

Ideas for Parents and Teachers

Pogo Books let children practice reading informational text while introducing them to nonfiction features such as headings, labels, sidebars, maps, and diagrams, as well as a table of contents, glossary, and index.

Carefully leveled text with a strong photo match offers early fluent readers the support they need to succeed.

Before Reading

- "Walk" through the book and point out the various nonfiction features. Ask the student what purpose each feature serves.
- Look at the glossary together. Read and discuss the words.

Read the Book

- Have the child read the book independently.
- Invite him or her to list questions that arise from reading.

After Reading

- Discuss the child's questions. Talk about how he or she might find answers to those questions.
- Prompt the child to think more. Ask: Have you ever seen a web or another structure made by a spider? Did you see the spider building it?

Pogo Books are published by Jump!
5357 Penn Avenue South
Minneapolis, MN 55419
www.jumplibrary.com

Library of Congress Cataloging-in-Publication Data

Names: Kenney, Karen Latchana, author.
Title: Spiders / by Karen Latchana Kenney.
Description: Minneapolis, MN: Jump! Inc., [2017]
Series: Animal architects | "Pogo Books are published by Jump!" | Audience: Ages 7-10. | Includes index.
Identifiers: LCCN 2016054733 (print)
LCCN 2016055483 (ebook)
ISBN 9781620316962 (hardcover: alk. paper)
ISBN 9781624965739 (ebook)
Subjects: LCSH: Spiders—Juvenile literature.
Spider webs—Juvenile literature.
Classification: LCC QL458.4 .K458 2017 (print)
LCC QL458.4 (ebook) | DDC 595.4/4—dc23
LC record available at https://lccn.loc.gov/2016054733

Editor: Kirsten Chang
Book Designer: Michelle Sonnek
Photo Researcher: Michelle Sonnek

Photo Credits: blickwinkel/Alamy, cover; Audrey Snider-Bell/Shutterstock, 1; Meister Photos/Shutterstock, 3; Eric Isselee/Shutterstock, 4; rotofrank/iStock, 5; Cathy Keifer/Shutterstock, 6-7; pattara puttiwong/Shutterstock, 8-9; Kirsanov Valeriy Vladimirovich/Shutterstock, 10-11; FloralImages/Alamy, 12; Stephen Dalton/Nature Picture Library, 13; Darlyne A. Murawski/Getty, 14-15; Ch'ien Lee/SuperStock, 16-17; JD Leeds/Shutterstock, 18; Steve Hopkin/age fotostock, 19; Andy Hall/Getty, 20-21; KANCHANA DUANGPANTA/Shutterstock, 23.

Printed in the United States of America at Corporate Graphics in North Mankato, Minnesota.

TABLE OF CONTENTS

CHAPTER 1

A STICKY TRAP

It's night. An orb weaver spider begins its web. First it releases a silky string into the wind. The string sticks from one plant to another. The spider crawls to the middle of the strand.

It strings silk from the center, like spokes on a bicycle. It connects the strands with more silk. Soon it has built a sticky spiral. The spider waits in the middle. An insect will fly right into this sticky trap.

A spider is not an insect, like an ant. It is an **arachnid**. It has two body sections. At the front are two jaws. Each jaw ends in a sharp fang.

All spiders are **predators**. They eat insects. Their silk helps them catch their **prey**. They use silk to build webs of different shapes and sizes. Their webs are great traps.

Webs are hard to see. Some strings are sticky. Some are not. An insect easily gets stuck. But spiders know which strings aren't sticky.

A spider's body helps it build. See its eight legs? It can crawl almost anywhere. It can move up trees and across ceilings, too.

More than 43,000 kinds of spiders live on Earth. They live everywhere except Antarctica.

All spiders make their own building material. Spider silk starts as a liquid inside a spider's **abdomen**. It hardens and comes out of **spinnerets**. Now it is a thread.

Spider silk is strong and stretchy. It can be sticky, too. Spiders can use silk to make many structures.

spinnerets

abdomen

CHAPTER 2

···

BUILDING WITH SILK

Some spiders make funnel webs. These webs have two parts. There is a flat sheet web connected to a small web tunnel.

tunnel

sheet web

The spider hides in the tunnel and waits. Soon an insect gets trapped on the sheet web. The spider comes out to grab its meal. Then the spider hurries back into the tunnel to eat.

A spider's web can even be a tool. The net-casting spider uses its web like a net. It weaves a rectangular web. It holds the web in its front four legs while hanging from a strand of silk. When an insect comes near, the spider drops its web. The insect gets tangled inside.

TAKE A LOOK!

There are many different kinds of spider webs.

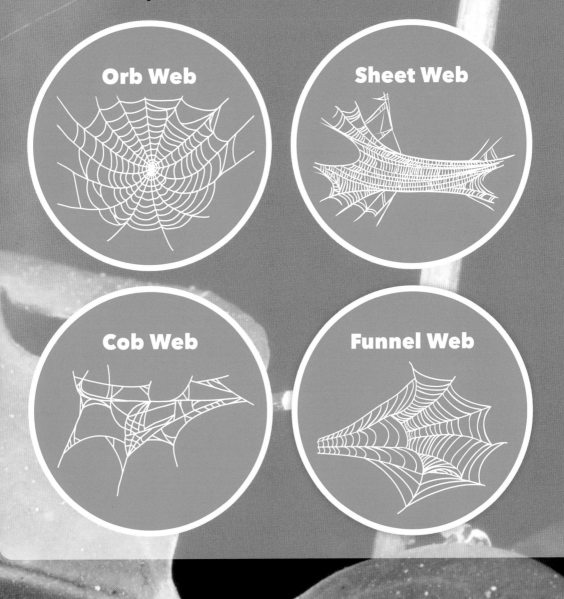

Orb Web

Sheet Web

Cob Web

Funnel Web

Some spiders don't make webs. A **tarantula** digs a **burrow** in the ground. It digs side **chambers**, too.

The spider lines the tunnel and chambers with stiff silk. This makes the burrow strong. It hides inside. It waits for insects to come near. Then it attacks.

DID YOU KNOW?

Trapdoor spiders make burrows. They add a door made from silk and dirt. The door blends in with the ground.

CHAPTER 3

· ·

HELPFUL SPIDERS

Look around your house. Can you find a spider web? Spiders can live in a home all year long.

Some people are afraid of spiders. But spider webs trap insects in homes. They catch flies, bed bugs, and other pests.

Scientists want to learn more about spider silk. They study it. They want to make something just as strong and stretchy. It could be made into strong ropes. Or it could be used in bandages for wounds.

Spinning strong silk and weaving webs, spiders are always busy building.

ACTIVITIES & TOOLS

COMPARE WEBS

Find and study spider webs in this activity.

What You Need:
- spider webs
- notebook
- pencil
- camera (optional)
- computer (optional)

❶ Go outside early in the morning with an adult. Look for spider webs on bushes or plants. Find at least two.

❷ Draw the webs on paper, or take pictures with your camera.

❸ If you cannot find webs outside, look on the Internet for pictures. Find two pictures of different webs.

❹ Look at the webs. How are they the same? How are they different? Write your thoughts on a piece of paper.

❺ Review what you wrote. Why do you think the webs have different shapes?

abdomen: The back section of a spider's body.

arachnid: A creature with a body divided into two parts, such as a spider or a scorpion.

burrow: A hole in the ground where a creature can live.

chambers: Large rooms.

predators: Animals that hunt and eat other animals.

prey: An animal that is hunted by other animals for food.

spinnerets: Organs which a spider uses to spin silk.

tarantula: A large poisonous spider from tropical America.

TO LEARN MORE

Learning more is as easy as 1, 2, 3.

1) Go to www.factsurfer.com

2) Enter "spiderarchitects" into the search box.

3) Click the "Surf" button to see a list of websites.

With factsurfer, finding more information is just a click away.